PUT IN WORK

Gain Respect, Influence Others, and Get Results as a New Leader

Brandi M. Baldwin, PhD

LEADER-ISH PUBLISHING
www.leader-ish.com

ISBN-13: 978-1696882835

Printed in the United States of America

SECOND EDITION

To the high-achievers, dreamers, visionaries, go-getters, innovators, and trend-setters who understand that true leadership is about making unpopular decisions, going against the grain, and fighting for what is right. Strive to show humble strength, integrity, and respect for the position you have been given; for you have the power to change the world.

CONTENTS

PREFACE

Leadership isn't all that it's cracked up to be... if you're doing it right. It's tough, unrewarding, lonely, stressful, and scary most of the time. And what gets me is that there's no easy way to figure out if you're an effective leader or not. You can read as many leadership and management books as you want, and take as many assessments as you think you need, and still guide your organization and its people down the wrong path. The truth is, there's just you and the people you serve—the people who expect you to answer their questions, cater for their concerns, make problems go away, and make their lives easier. And according to the numbers, 64% of new leaders don't make it more than 18 months before quitting or being fired.

So, why even bother being a leader? Why bother with the headaches and stress? Why bother coming in early and leaving late? Why risk missing time with your family? Carrying the heavy load of everyone else's work and your own? Why? Is it because of the money? Is it because of the title? Is it to feed your own ego? Hopefully not.

Hopefully, it's because of the challenge, the thrill, and the opportunity to make a positive change in a place that would be worse off without you. Hopefully, you're there to leave your mark. Hopefully, you want to be a leader because deep down inside you've always been a leader; whether you had the formal title or not. That's it. That's exactly it. *You* are it. You are reading this book because you know that you are *"it"*—that leader, that change-agent, that star, that renegade, that innovator, that go-getter. You know that you're already *good* at leadership, but in this season of your career, you want to be *great.* You want to be your best, and you're tired of doing this thing called leadership on your own. You're tired of figuring it out as you go along. You've had some wins, and you know that even a few of those losses could've been avoided, if only you had someone by your side to help you navigate your leadership journey. Well, guess what? Here I am. It's not the book who's talking to you, it's me, Dr. Brandi, and if it's alright with you, I'd like to hire myself as your personal leadership advisor. My job is to push you, and help you question your assumptions about your role as a leader. It's to tell you the ugly truth about what you're getting yourself into when it comes to building your leadership brand. As we work together, I'll share personal stories and my own leadership lessons. You'll have assignments to complete and goals to set, and together we'll work to take your leadership competence to the next level.

I want to be clear, though. **Put in Work** is not a textbook, nor is it a reference manual. I'm not here to wow you with research, statistics, and theoretical musings. This book is a practical guide that will inspire you to step your game up as a leader. If you do the work, you'll see an amazing breakthrough in your professional life. If you don't do the work, you'll be exactly where you are today—*good*, but not *great* as a leader.

Now, since we're getting to know one another, I'd like to start by sharing with you the greatest lesson I've learned (thus far) about leadership.

What Got You Here Won't Get You There

For starters, I wasn't born into a wealthy family, and I didn't grow up in a wealthy town. And by sharing that we weren't wealthy, I really mean, we were straight up poor. I'm talking run the oven to heat the house poor. I'm talking spam, kool-aid, and ramen noodles poor. I'm talking dollar movies, and sharing happy meals with my mom poor. We didn't have *things*, but we had each other. Our "poor-people problems" actually helped to build my character. I didn't have the luxury of worrying about the latest toys and clothes, and all of the superficial things that define who children are today. I was worried about me and who I was as a person. I was focused on figuring out what I needed to do to get to where "those other people" were. Those people I saw on television; those people with influence, power, and respect. I wanted some of that, and I was *just* self-centered and naive enough to believe that it could actually be done. At eight years old, I already knew that I was destined for greatness.

Unfortunately, what I knew in my mind was a lot different from what I saw in my reality. My teenage mom worked around the clock to pay the bills and keep food on the table. I was your typical latchkey kid, coming home to an empty house on most days, doing and checking my own homework, cooking dinner, cleaning the house, and writing out the bills

(I can balance a checkbook like nobody's business!). I was the second in command at home, and my mom was the Chief Drill Sergeant. It was just the two of us, and she made sure to train me (her little lieutenant) right. She had me washing baseboards, working on my penmanship, typing on the typewriter, clipping coupons, and doing laundry.

She'd check my work and if there was one mistake, she'd make me start from scratch and do it all over again. I'd be rolling my eyes, sucking my teeth, holding back tears, and praying for God to give me a break! But no, I never really got a break. In many ways, I didn't get a full chance to be a child. Don't get me wrong; at the time, I was content, but looking back at it, I remember being stressed out, scared, and on edge for a good part of my childhood. I had a lot of responsibilities, but I can only imagine how stressful it was for my mom to raise me all by herself. No wonder she was on me like white on rice! She was and is my very best friend.

We had this special knock so that I'd know when it was safe to answer the door. She taught me a secret ring for when she called the house so that I knew it was okay to answer the phone.

The silver lining of my life was school. I loved going to school because it was *my* domain. I was a winner when I was at school. By middle school, I'd transformed into your classic high-achieving student: president of the student government, always on the honor roll, perfect attendance, dubbed "talented and gifted," track star, orchestra nerd, and entrepreneur (I made a couple hundred dollars a month tutoring friends, publishing my own monthly newsletter, walking dogs, and doing nails for my girlfriends). You name it, I did it. When I was at school, everything I touched turned to gold. I was a dancer, athlete, violinist, and honors student. I could hang with the cool kids, chill with the jocks, and kick it with the nerds. I was well-rounded, likeable, and moderately popular. I graduated from high school with a 4.20 GPA and I got accepted into a large state college a few hours away in Philadelphia. By then, my mother was married, we had "moved on up to the east side." We were living comfortably in the middle class suburbs of Maryland right outside of Washington, DC. I was ready to head off to college, repeat my success, and conquer the real world. That was my plan and I knew I'd be nothing less than successful. Unfortunately, for me, what I expected and what happened were two different things.

In college, I got a serious wake-up call. Back home, I was all that, but in college, I was mediocre at best. I struggled in class and worked twice as hard to get A's. I was back at the bottom as a starving student, (moms cut me off with the quickness once I left the house). I worked three jobs to make ends meet. I worked at the temp agency during the day, at The Gap until the mall closed, and at this cool little Puerto Rican bar on Fridays and Saturdays. I was working harder than ever before. What worked for me in high school wasn't working for me in college. I had to find a new set of skills to succeed in this new environment. That's when I learned my biggest leadership lesson: **what works for you on one level, won't work for you on the next.** In other words, what got you to where you are today won't get you where you need to be tomorrow.

Just for one second, I want you to think about your life as it is today. In what areas are you feeling stuck? What areas of your life aren't thriving like they used to? Those are the exact areas where you need to upgrade your approach. Change, adjust, adapt, transform, and evolve. What worked for you before isn't working now and you are in control of making the necessary changes that will bring you new, better results. Once I learned that lesson, my adult life was dramatically changed. Instead of working three jobs, I got a promotion and only had to work one. I bought my first home at 23. I started my first company by 25. Instead of struggling to get my undergraduate degree, I moved on to attend graduate school and ultimately earned a PhD by the age of 30. Not because I was *all that*, but because I was smart enough to change my *methods* as I reached each new level in life.

Don't Be a High-Achieving Failure

I need you to hear this, and hear it good. The strategies that you have employed to be successful in your previous position will not help you become successful in your next position. That's right. **The strategies that you have employed to be successful in your previous position will not help you become successful in your next position.** What they will do, however, is help you to become a high-achieving failure. Someone who is good at what they're good at, and terrible at everything else.

You know that you're a high-achieving failure if you're experiencing lack in one or more areas of your life. Where you were once able to execute, you aren't executing anymore. Where you were once getting stellar results, you're no longer hitting the mark. Where you were once lauded and appreciated, you're no longer getting respect. Where you were once content and happy, you're no longer confident and excited. It was easy back then wasn't it? Back when you were "on top"? To the average person, you're still on top. You have the title, education, and every once in a while you get a public "win". But in private, you know that you're not as effective as you once were. What's scarier is that you aren't as effective now as you need to be to take your career and life to the next level. It's time to get off of the hamster wheel so you can reach the next level success.

Take Your Career to the Next Level

As the leader of your life and organization, you need to gain or regain the respect of important others, increase your influence, and execute on a level that brings results on a consistent basis. You have to solve people's problems in your own unique way. The bottom line is that you have to increase your value *now*. If you're stuck in one or more areas of your life, this book will help you figure out where those areas are and what you can do day-in and day-out to execute at a whole new level.

This book is for you if you aspire to be a leader or if you're already a leader, but you need to take a hard look at the level of your impact. Whether you're starting out or fairly seasoned, this book is what you need, not to *learn* more about leadership, but to *apply* leadership strategies to your daily practice. As you get into the meat of the book, I encourage you to reach out to me directly with your ideas, and personal questions. I can be reached directly at **contact@doctorbrandi.com**. Over the last few years I've worked one-on-one with over 1,500 professionals helping them take their careers to the next level, and I'm excited to help you do the same. Let's get started!

-Dr. Brandi

INTRODUCTION

You can *win* as a leader if you commit your daily practice to a few simple things. This book is all about helping you elevate your leadership performance in six key areas: **branding, emotional competence, conflict management, communication, organizational politics, and strategic execution.**

Gain Respect, Influence Others, and Get Results

Gaining respect, influencing others, and getting results are the three toughest challenges that leaders face. In each chapter, I will address each of these major leadership challenges and you will have an opportunity to craft specific goals around developing each area. This book is about taking action and changing your behavior, so make sure to complete each of the action plans.

Each of the performance areas build upon the idea that to be an effective new leader, you have to create your own unique blend of interpersonal skills and practices so that you can perform at your best. This isn't a one-sized-fits-all framework. It's actually not a framework at all. It's a starting point to reassess how well you are managing your leadership brand.

Each chapter is designed to educate, inspire, motivate, and guide you through your leadership development journey. You'll notice that every chapter is organized into eight different sections: *leader-isms, what you need to know, take two, the tough stuff, the secret to success, 60-day action plan, don't fear,* and *personalize it.* Here's a quick description of what each section has to offer.

Leader-isms

Each chapter begins with a **"leader-ism"** that relates to each leadership practice. You might as well call it a Dr. Brandi-ism because it's the key take-away that I want you to have. It's a leadership commandment of sorts.

What You Need to Know

This section is exactly what I want you to know about the leadership practice being discussed. I'll define key terms and briefly orient you to the concept, but I won't go deep. If you're looking for scholarly articles and references, you won't get it here. What you will get is just enough context to help you understand the essence of the leadership practice being discussed.

Take Two

In this section you will find two actions to take right away. These "starter" strategies are the foundation for where you should begin improving your leadership habits.

The Tough Stuff

Most books make you feel like following leadership "best practices" will always yield positive results. Honestly, nothing is guaranteed to do that, so I thought it'd be helpful to give you some key insights on how to anticipate common challenges. If you know what to expect, you'll have a better chance of managing setbacks as they occur.

The Secret to Success

The secret to success section is a single non-negotiable action that is critical to the successful integration of your new leadership practice. It may be an action that you need to take or a mindset that you need to have to increase your chances of successfully mastering each practice. These secrets are designed to help your efforts "stick" once you put them to the test.

60-Day Action Plan

What's the use of learning about leadership habits if you don't take action? But what exactly are you supposed to do first? In this section, I provide you with key behaviors and actions that you need to implement within the first 60-days of upgrading your leadership.

Don't Fear

In this section I provide you with encouragement as you embark on your leadership journey. Before I throw you to the wolves, I'll give you one last boost to help you *win* at implementing your new leadership practice.

Personalize It

This is your opportunity to identify specific actions you will take to upgrade your leadership capacity. This section is where you identify when, who, and how you will incorporate your new leadership practices within the context of your professional organization.

But Wait, There's More

In the back of the book, you will find a Leadership Implementation Guide. It's a self-discovery tool that I created to accelerate your leadership right away.

As you read through the book, pull lessons from your own life to customize the learning experience for yourself. Take notes, ask questions, and invite colleagues to join you in upgrading their leadership performance.

Final Thoughts

You and I both know that you are different. You are a leader. You're a part of a club, a group of people who want to have an impact on the world. You know that things are not as good as they can be. You've tried before to influence others, accelerate your success, and up-level your game, but now, the stakes are even higher. You need to perform at your best to take your organization to the next level. Your reputation needs to open doors for you. Your career must continue to grow. This book is designed to help you take a deeper look at yourself. The ultimate goal is to give you what you need to take action in a new and more productive way. Answer the call. Accept the challenge. Lead your career to the next level today. Turn the page, and begin the next chapter of your leadership journey… with me.

PART ONE

GAIN RESPECT

GET CLEAR ABOUT YOUR LEADERSHIP BRAND

Leader-Ism #1: Your Brand Is What People Say About You When You're Not Around

The Weekend Supervisor Job from Hell

I was in my early twenties and had just started my doctoral program studying Educational Leadership and Policy. I taught classes part-time at a local college to make ends meet. On top of that, I was a new mom and needed a flexible work schedule to accommodate the surgeries, doctor's appointments, and therapy sessions for my newborn daughter, who was born with a rare health condition.

I just knew my full-time employer would understand my need for a flexible schedule. But after putting in a formal request, I got an email from my supervisor who told me to "feel free to look for other employment options." I was like, "oh no he didn't!" But, oh yes he did, and I had two months to find a new full-time job that fit with my schedule… and bank account. Sure enough, I found a job posted online for a Weekend Supervisor at a residential mental health treatment home. I had experience in behavioral health and knew that I was qualified, so I applied and was hired right away! My hours were 7am-7pm Friday, Saturday, and Sunday, and I'd be on call 24/7 every weekend. The schedule worked for me, and I was excited to start supervising. Little did I know, I wouldn't get much supervising done at all.

I soon realized that this would be the job from hell. I loved the residential setting. I'm a natural helper so I couldn't wait to come in and help the residents stay motivated to achieve their daily and weekly goals. But there was something "off" about this place.

To start, the leadership consisted of a director who always "disappeared" for random meetings and appointments. The program manager took so many smoke breaks; I'm surprised she got any work done. The other supervisors were pretty cool, but had their own little quirks. The residents were a blessing to work with (except the one who attacked me with a boom box and a curtain rod…long story). There was never a dull moment, and young, naïve, over-confident, overly optimistic me would soon have a rude awakening.

To cut to the chase, I didn't fit in… in the worst way. I stuck out like a sore thumb, and looking back at it, I know why. I had no idea that I never branded myself as a leader. I came in as the young, bubbly, graduate student. I was more concerned with making friends than making tough decisions and instead of commanding authority, I commanded laughter. I could barely get anyone to take me seriously. I was acknowledged as a hard worker and someone who people wanted to be around, but when it came to making tough decisions, my authority was always usurped by a more senior member of the front-line staff. I had no authority whatsoever.

Seniority is what really mattered at this job, and 59 year old Darlene gave me a speech every week about the fact that she had been there for twenty years and "could run the place with her eyes closed." According to her, she never "went up" for the weekend supervisor position because it didn't work with her schedule. "I can't be giving up my weekends girl!" she'd say. After a few weeks, no joke, she had me doing *her* job! I felt like I was *her* assistant. I was a leader with a title, and no actual respect, and that's because I didn't have a clear leadership brand.

What You Need to Know

Gaining respect as a new leader can be challenging. People are expecting you to perform on a higher level, and everything you say and do is scrutinized by your team, peers, and superiors. Having a distinct leadership brand is critical to your success as a high-performing leader. In this chapter, we'll discuss what a leadership brand is and why it matters to your performance as a new leader. I also want to share some of the challenges you're bound to face as you refine your leadership brand on the job. You'll walk away with specific steps to take to establish and refine your own leadership brand.

Your leadership title is more than where you are on the organizational chart. That title means that you have more power, and *much* more to prove than someone without it. Being a high-achieving employee and newly appointed leader are two different things that require two different strategies. Remember, what got you the leadership title, won't help you keep it.

So, the obvious question is: what exactly is a leadership brand? It's simple. Think of it as your identity as a leader; who you are as a leader within your organization, what you stand for, how you make people feel, and how you handle your business. Whether you've thought about it or not, you already have a leadership brand. Just ask your coworkers for feedback about how you interact with others, solve problems, and execute tasks.

Your leadership brand is what people say about you when you're not around. So, think about it. How would your last client describe you? What would one of your colleagues say about your integrity, and decision-making abilities? How would your supervisor describe your management style? Your leadership brand is who you are as a leader, distinct and different from whom you were as a non-leader. That slight difference matters when it comes to how you will earn and sustain respect in your new role.

There are a few questions you can answer as you develop your leadership brand. As you read through each of them, write down some initial answers. Don't ask friends, family, or colleagues to help you with this. Think deeply about each question on your own to create the most authentic leadership brand possible. Remember, this process is about being reflective about who you are when you're on the job. Don't attempt to create a leadership brand of perfection that you won't be able to maintain for more than a few weeks. Think about the unique aspects of your personality that are critical to your success in this position.

- What is important to me as a leader?
- What is important to my team?
- What value do I offer?
- What will people experience when interacting with me?
- How do I want people to feel after meeting or interacting with me?
- What do I want to be known for?
- What type of communicator do I want to be?

After brainstorming responses to each question, you should be left with a comprehensive list of adjectives, phrases, and ideas that you can use to craft your leadership brand. For additional help, flip back to section one of the Implementation Guide found in the back of this book.

Don't attempt to create your leadership brand overnight. It can take 2-3 weeks to create something that feels doable, authentic, and real. Once you've refined your ideas, think about the actions and behaviors that are in alignment with each of your leadership brand characteristics. It is through consistent behavior that you are going to solidify your leadership brand.

Take Two

Two things to remember as you practice this leadership skill.

1. Start With Your Strengths

You're already pretty awesome! I know because you're reading this book (wink). That said, start with your strengths when it comes to developing your leadership brand. What are you already good at? What professional compliments do others give you without hesitation? What are you already known for? Those personal characteristics should definitely make the list when it comes to developing your leadership brand. Many people think they have to become a whole new person, but that's not true. Be you, but be the best you, as a leader with a formal title.

2. Fake it 'Til You Make It

When you're clear about your leadership brand, you may have to evoke your inner actor or actress. There will be times when you're going to have to fake it until your new brand becomes second nature. If you're usually not personable, but you want to be seen as someone who is more approachable at work, put that smile on the next time someone knocks on your office door and interrupts your lunch. And speaking of lunch, spend it with your colleagues instead of cooped up in your office. Even if you're not there yet, fake it. You may be Debbie Downer on Friday, but come in as Upbeat Ellen on Monday and never look back!

The Tough Stuff

Creating your leadership brand sounds easy enough, but there are some things that can derail your entire plan. Let's talk about them.

Launching Your *New* Brand within the Same Company

Going from non-leader to leader within the same company can get a little tricky. First, your colleagues and coworkers are used to the non-leader version of you. Changing the perceptions of others can be difficult and frustrating, especially on the job.

As you're getting used to your new role as a leader, you may notice that important others are still interacting with the "old" you. Maybe they're still expecting you to "hook them up" in a time of need. Maybe they're not respecting your authority. Maybe they're just not ready to see you as a leader. All of that is okay, and will happen at some point during your transition. You may even find that the very people who promoted you, aren't engaging with you in a way that respects your new leadership brand.

The question still remains: what do you do when your efforts to establish a leadership brand are thwarted because your coworkers can't help but see the "old" you? The answer is simple: be consistent. Consistency is your best friend when establishing a new professional brand and reputation. Day in and day out, communicate, engage, and make decisions in ways that are consistent with the new ways in which you want people to perceive you. Over time, your consistent behavior will "stick" in the minds of your colleagues. My mom always told me, "You train people how to treat you." That same principal applies here. Train your colleagues to treat you as the respected leader you are.

Leadership Brand and Company Culture Mismatch

It can be tough to establish a new leadership brand for yourself when it doesn't jive with the current company culture. Take this scenario for example: you're excited about your new leadership brand, and you waltz in to work on Monday to start your 60-day brand implementation process. You spoke up in the morning meeting, you gave some tough feedback to one of your team members, and you gave a compliment to a colleague you haven't been seeing eye-to-eye with. You're killing it! But by lunch time you're getting weird looks, maybe even a few questions, and you're feeling silly. You realize that your new and improved leadership brand is inconsistent with the company culture. You're sticking out like a sore thumb and you feel like it'll be easier to just "fit in."

Well, you're right; it would be easier to fit in to the company culture, but it'll be more rewarding to stay committed to your leadership brand. Some of your new behaviors may not be valued or accepted at first, but it's still your responsibility to do what's best for your professional advancement and the company. Use your current opportunity to sharpen your leadership skills. See what works and what doesn't work, make adjustments, and become confident in who you are as a leader. Changing your leadership brand to fit in with the company culture is like aiming for a moving target. Chances are, you'll miss the mark and never feel secure in your leadership identity.

The Secret to Success

Stay Consistent

I can't emphasize enough the importance of staying consistent with the implementation of your brand. Don't deviate, don't apologize, and don't get lazy. Boldly present your best self and stick with it until it becomes second nature. Get an accountability partner who can help you work through your challenges during the first 60-days of implementing your new brand strategy.

60-Day Implementation Plan

There's some prep work that needs to be done before presenting your new leadership brand to the world (and by the world, I mean at your job). Once you've answered the discovery questions in this chapter, complete Section One of the Implementation Guide. It will help you identify key words that represent your leadership brand.

Your final leadership brand should be 5-7 behaviors or characteristics that you want to include in your daily professional practice. Don't attempt to incorporate 10 new behaviors into your leadership brand. Think of your leadership brand as an extension of your professional (non-leadership) brand. That is, who you were as a professional before you got the promotion. Your leadership brand is not a new persona or alter ego. It's your best self as a leadership professional. It's all of your most relevant strengths wrapped up in one attractive package for your colleagues to enjoy. For the next 60 days, follow these simple steps and make adjustments as necessary.

Day 1 to Day 30

Take as many opportunities as possible to behave in ways that are consistent with your new leadership brand. If you want to be perceived as a direct communicator, every chance that you get to communicate with someone individually or in a small group, be direct! It's just that simple. During this first week, select a characteristic that is already a part of who you are as a professional. If you're already personable, and want to keep that as a part of your leadership brand, continue that behavior during week one.

During week two, I want you to introduce another leadership characteristic into your daily practice. Remember to continue behaving in ways that are consistent with your week one characteristic, while also adding your week two characteristic into the routine. For this week, select a leadership trait that is not a part of your normal practice; something that will feel different and be a challenge.

For weeks three and four, continue the pattern above. During week three, implement a leadership characteristic that's "easy" and already a natural part of who you are. During week four, implement a leadership characteristic that is more difficult or "new". Remember that with each new week, you are still behaving in ways that are consistent with your week one, two, and three practices. Each week should build off of the last.

Week five is critical. It's a checkpoint where I want you to do a few things to monitor your progress thus far. During week five, I want you to continue to observe how people are interacting with you and look for clues that can tell you if you're getting it right or getting it wrong. Are you building stronger relationships with your team? Are you getting more respect? Are people valuing your opinion a lot more? Take a step back and begin to assess the impact of your leadership brand and be prepared to make some changes along the way.

Day 31 to Day 60

During weeks six through eight, introduce the last two to three leadership characteristics into your daily practice. Remember that at this point, your leadership brand is becoming more refined and nuanced. The goal is for your brand to be on autopilot. It should become a part of who you are day-in and day-out.

Finally, during week eight, ask for feedback about the "new" you. Don't make a big deal about it; don't set up formal meetings with people. Simply ask three to four of your colleagues for informal (and impromptu) feedback about how you're doing. See if they are able to identify some of your leadership characteristics without you telling them about your changes. Use their feedback to make necessary adjustments. If people seem indifferent about the "new" you, or, if they are unable to clearly articulate changes they've noticed, you're not being assertive enough in your approach. Kick it up a notch and make some *noticeable* positive behavior changes.

If you're nervous about how to ask for feedback, that's okay, blame it on me. You can say that your "leadership advisor" gave you an assignment and you wanted to see if they could help you out. Ask your colleagues to use three words to describe you and see what they come up with. What you hear will be exactly what you need to make an informed decision about your next steps.

Don't Fear

Establishing a leadership brand is critical to your professional success. As you embark on this leadership journey, **don't fear stepping too far outside of your comfort zone.** When you step outside of your comfort zone, you'll scare folks, make others uncomfortable, and (if you're doing it right) scare the mess out of yourself!

That's right! Expect this process to be uncomfortable and understand that being a leader has less to do with your technical expertise and more to do with how you relate to others in your network. I know some smart leaders who have the title, but not one true follower within their organization, all because they don't have a polished leadership brand.

Gaining respect is all about consistently being your best. This doesn't mean you have to be perfect, but you do have to show up ready and willing to work, and do the things you say you're going to do. In leadership, gaining followers is not like social media. You don't have to entertain, amuse, or impress your team; you just need to perform at your best and add value to their professional experience. If you can do that, you'll be in good shape. For now, hone in on your leadership brand and design it to get the maximum benefit for your life and career.

Personalize It

Now that we've discussed your leadership brand, I want you to personalize your 60-day implementation plan. Be specific and identify each trait that you'll implement during each week. Also, identify the key behaviors you'll need to enact in order to successfully implement your re-branding strategy.

Week #	Brand Characteristic	On-the-Job Actions
1		
2		
3		
4		
5		
6		
7		
8		

2

GET YOUR EMOTIONS
IN CHECK

Leader-Ism #2: Never Let Them See You Sweat

The Lesson My Schizophrenic Client Taught Me

Ever see the movie *Silence of the Lambs* with Sir Anthony Hopkins? If you haven't, definitely make it a Netflix night and watch when you get a chance. It'll make this story all the more relevant. Well, if you've seen the movie, you know about the scenes where Clarice goes to visit Hannibal Lector at a correctional facility for the "criminally insane." She walks down this long dark hallway in the basement of the facility and as she passes each cell, inmates grab at her, lick their tongues out at her, and whisper nasty things. It's really a bit gruesome. But in a few short moments she finally arrives at Hannibal Lector's cell. He's inside wearing an orange jumpsuit with his back facing her. Before they even make eye contact, he starts talking. He names the perfume she's wearing and begins analyzing her mood. As a young detective, she's stunned at his ability to "read" her, even before he's seen her face. She was terrified to be left alone with him, but she did whatever she needed to do to get help for her case. And so, for the next several years she works together with Mr. Lector to solve serial killings in the area. Although he was "insane" himself, he taught Clarice many things about herself, and in my mid-twenties I had a job just like that! Minus the detective work, serial killings, and FBI clearance… okay so maybe it wasn't exactly the same, but just follow me here.

I was a behavioral health coordinator (a.k.a. social worker) who helped people independently reintegrate back into the community after suffering from mental health setbacks. I remember one client, Terry, who was being released from the local state hospital in a few weeks. I was assigned as her new case manager, and from what I was told, she hated all of her previous case managers and wasn't too fond of the guards and staff at the state hospital. This particular hospital was a maximum security facility for people with severe mental health conditions. She was diagnosed with schizophrenia and couldn't get a grasp on reality on most days. Word on the street (and by the street I mean in her case file) was that she was prone to violence, easily agitated, and known to have emotional outbursts. I can remember like yesterday, the day I met her for the first time.

When I visited the facility for her discharge meeting, I laid eyes on her for the first time. I swear she had to be six feet tall with a football player's frame. I'm about 115lbs soaking wet and to me, she looked like a giant… actually, she looked like a man, but either way she was *big*. After the meeting with Terry's treatment team, I was offered "alone time" with her. I was locked inside of a small dark room, with no window, dim gray lights, and one flimsy wooden table with various words etched into its fibers. I glanced back at the guard one last time and he gave me a quick wink to let me know everything would be okay. Oh yea, can't forget to mention that there was a bright red "emergency phone" hanging on the wall about fifteen feet away from where I was sitting. I immediately started making a game-plan just in case things went south. I thought to myself, "if I do a ninja kick to knock the table over, and slide across the floor, I can get to the phone in less than three seconds". All I could think about was the movie Silence of the Lambs.

There I was, staring Terry in the face with a huge nervous smile. My underarms were pouring sweat, and I felt a slight twinge of nausea from the mix of funk and stale cigarette smoke emanating from her clothes. For the next seven minutes, which felt like an hour, I listened intently to her talk in circles about horses, and space ships, the CIA, and something about people trying to get her. She sounded crazy, but I understood that in this room, in this hospital, I was in *her* world. So I played along. She would pause here and there and I'd fill in with a well-placed ad lib, "Mmm hmm, is that right? Really? I can't believe that!"

By the end of our time together, she was reaching over to give me a hug! I'll never forget what she told me before I left. She said, "The other people in here treat me like I'm crazy. I've been telling them that I'm fine and that I don't belong here. You're the first person who listened to me and understood what I was saying." Between you and I, the truth is: I didn't have a clue what she was talking about during our conversation. But as I thought about the underlying meaning of her statement, I learned a valuable lesson about emotional competence and its power to gain the respect of others. What I did *right* in that situation was, I adjusted my emotional reactions to match what made Terry feel comfortable. I was in her territory, and by adjusting my emotional reactions, she perceived me as understanding her on a deeper level.

For the next several months, Terry and I became great pals. She moved into her own apartment, and became self-sufficient. I'd accompany her on visits to the psychiatrist and therapist and time after time, I'd witness doctors and social workers trying to "snap" her out of her reality. "Terry, now that's not true is it?" "Terry hun, what you're saying doesn't make any sense." Rather than trying to pull her back into my world, I took a step into her world every time we were together.

Building emotional competence is the same way. You have to immerse yourself in the environment around you and adhere to the social rules of engagement for where you are. The same is true for getting your emotions in check as a leader.

As a new leader, you must get and keep your emotions in check right away. People will test you, get on your nerves, get under your skin, and blatantly disrespect you. You have to be equipped with the skills to overcome the emotional roller coaster of leadership. While others around you may be emotionally immature, you won't get the same "pass" that they will. You don't have the luxury of losing your cool in a meeting, or crossing the line out of anger or frustration. You set the tone and the example for what is acceptable within your organization. I don't care if your supervisor or the entire executive team is emotionally immature, that doesn't mean you can behave in the same way. Your emotional competence is an important part of your leadership brand. How you manage and display your emotions will determine how quickly you'll gain respect within your organization.

What You Need to Know

Emotional competence is your ability to recognize your own (and other people's) emotions. Once you recognize the emotion, you can label it and use that information to appropriately guide your thinking and behavior. People who are emotionally competent are able to adjust their behaviors in different situations and with different people.

Context is everything when it comes to emotional competence. You wouldn't interact with a colleague in the same way that you would interact with your best friend. You wouldn't behave at work in the same way that you behave at home, right? Some of us get caught up in being so "authentic" that we forget that it's necessary to adjust our behaviors to meet the needs of different situations. It's not about being fake or phony. The best leaders are conscious, aware, and purposeful about how they display their emotions in different situations. This interpersonal skill is a tool to build strategic relationships that can elevate your career and professional impact.

Enhancing your emotional competence can do wonders for your leadership brand and reputation. Many times we find ourselves engaging with people who are just like us. They talk like us, enjoy the same things we enjoy, and they understand the world through the same lens that we do. That makes us feel good, but it's not ideal as we enhance our leadership capabilities. Being emotionally competent gives us an opportunity to develop relationships with different kinds of people. That's what you want as a leader. You want to be able to hold a conversation with the janitor and the CEO. You want to be comfortable if you're the only person in the room with your background and experience. You may be the youngest, oldest, only male, or only female. You may be from a different culture. None of that will matter as you develop your emotional competence. You want to be able to move from situation to situation and blend right in. The only way you can do that, is by studying the way others interact in those situations. Learn the type of emotional responses that are valued. Study the rules of engagement and make a mental note so that you can walk the walk and talk the talk. Remember, still be you, but be ready to align your emotional presence to what is socially acceptable in the room. Developing your emotional competence isn't a hard science, it's an art.

When you're aware of your emotions, you can control how others perceive you. This is important when it comes to your leadership brand. Think about it. What do you want to be known for? Flying off the handle during staff meetings? Getting into an argument with a coworker? Barking orders to someone who supervise? Crying during a heated board meeting? People are learning about your leadership approach by assessing how you interact with others. Oh, and remember, people always talk. One bad interaction can ruin a reputation that you've worked hard to build.

A final note on emotional competence. You may be thinking, "I don't have time to change my emotional responses in every single situation. I am who I am; they can take it or leave it." I want to challenge you not to take the easy way out by using that approach. It's much easier (on the front end) to just "be yourself" everywhere you go. After a while however, you'll find it tough to build new relationships, find important allies, sustain respect in the workplace, and find new career opportunities. The more refined your emotional competence, the more access you'll have to professional opportunities. You don't want people to say, "No, I don't think he'll be right on that project," or "I doubt she'll be able to work with those type of people," or "He'll never do well in that environment". By proving that you are able to behave appropriately in different situations, you're proving to others that you are less concerned about yourself and more concerned with being your *best* self in front of important others.

Take Two

Two things to remember as you practice this leadership skill.

1. Get Trigger Happy

Later on in the chapter, I'll talk about emotional triggers; but for now, I have to bring it up as an essential part of building your emotional competence. Emotional triggers are events that happen which trigger specific emotions. In order to build your emotional competence over time, you must get trigger happy. That's right! Stay laser focused on the events, people, and situations that trigger negative emotional responses within you. Once you identify the things that get under your skin, you'll be able to create a plan for how to react when you encounter each situation.

2. Check Yourself

We're all adults here, right? You're going to have to hold yourself accountable from now on. No one's going to beg you to speak up in a board meeting; no one's going to put you in time-out if you fly off the handle at work. Most people won't bother pulling you aside and holding you accountable for your emotional behavior. Now's the time for you to start holding yourself accountable and changing any behaviors that don't serve your brand. Also, when you know you've had a set-back, check yourself, and make a plan so that it doesn't happen again. It's just that simple.

The Tough Stuff

Refining your emotional competence isn't easy. Here are some of the toughest things you'll encounter during the process of adjusting your emotional reactions.

Getting Rid of Old Habits

Our emotional reactions are ingrained in who we are. Most of the time, we're not thinking, "and now I'm going to scream at the receptionist." We just do it. The norms for how we should display emotions come from our home environment. Think about your mother and father, or whoever raised you. How did they behave when they were happy, angry, and frustrated? What types of behaviors did they accept as being "okay"? Were you allowed to show hurt, shame, or fear? Were you taught to cover up your negative emotions and pretend like everything was okay? All of our current habits were taught to us by others who were a part of our lives when we were children.

It's tough to shed old habits, but the first step is identifying the dysfunctional ways in which you react emotionally. Once you do that, you'll be able to design a plan to remove those behaviors that won't serve you as a leader.

Being Consistent

Changing your emotional reactions is all about consistency. You'll feel the urge to revert back to what you've always done, but make a conscious decision to display new emotional reactions for at least 60 days so that your new reactions can become ingrained within your psyche. People want to know that you'll show up the same way every time. When they see the consistency, they'll begin to trust you even more. Increased trust leads to increased respect in the workplace. Reconcile other's perception of you and you're on your way to gaining the respect of those you serve.

Learning New Ways to Process the Same Situations

Another tough part about building your emotional competence is learning how to react differently, not to new situations but to the same old situations that have challenged you in the past. For example, the next time the board meeting gets tense, instead of disengaging from the discussion, speak up and show that you're present. When someone who you don't get along with rubs you the wrong way, don't snap at them; try calmly explaining your point of view. One of the hardest things to do as you develop your emotional competence will be re-training yourself to change the way you react to common situations that you've been emotionally incompetent in before.

The Secret to Success

The secret to successfully developing your emotional competence is to change one negative emotional response at a time. Don't try to do it all at once. You'll fail miserably and people will think that you have a personality disorder. Identify all of the areas that you want to build your emotional competence and tackle them one at a time. I recommend spending a full month on changing on emotional reaction. You may say, "I want to change how I relate to my overly emotional boss." For the next 30-days, choose to interact differently with your boss. Be strategic about what you say, what you do, and how you react when you come in contact with him or her.

Remember, the purpose of elevating your emotional competence is not to become nicer. It's also not about getting others to like you or treat you differently than they already do. Some people will change how they interact with you because they begin to adjust to your new patterns of behavior. Others may behave in the exact same way that they do now, and that's okay. Increasing your emotional competence is about owning *your* emotions and being conscious and aware of how you are reacting in different contexts.

60-Day Implementation Plan

I'm not going to tell you what to do without giving you some guidance on how to do it. In this section, I'm going to lay out some key things that you need to do to assess your current dysfunctional emotional reactions, change unproductive emotional behaviors, and sustain new emotional responses that will serve you as a leader.

Day 1-30

The first month is all about self-assessment. The first thing you need to do is identify all of the destructive/unproductive emotions that you exhibit on the job. Make a list based off of how you've been behaving within the last 90 days. Don't be too hard on yourself. You shouldn't come up with a list of 20 different emotions. Identify five at the most.

Next, make a list of the challenging people and situations that you need to plan for. You're not going to be able to "wing it" and hope for the best. You're going to have to prepare for these people and the situations that you know will eventually trigger a negative emotional response from you. Once you identify each person or situation, go back to your first list and match each negative emotion that you identified to each person or situation. By so doing, you should get a better understanding of how these people and situations are negatively affecting your professional brand.

Finally, go a step further and identify the emotional triggers connected to each person and situation. That is, think about the specific things that they do to trigger a negative emotional response from you. Do they lie, raise their voice, or treat you like a child? Are the situations you identified stressful, time consuming, or perceived by you as a waste of time? Get to the root of why you have a negative reaction to each person or situation.

For the first thirty days, don't worry about jumping right in to changing your behaviors. Spend that time doing some deep self-reflection on why you react in certain ways. Once you do that work, it'll be much easier to elevate your emotional responses.

Day 31-60

The second month is all about taking action. The next thing I want you to do is create a plan for how you will react when you encounter each difficult person or challenging situation. What will you do or not do? What will you say? Be as specific as you can.

It'll also be helpful if you keep track of times that you digress as you're experimenting with new ways of interacting with others in different situations. Keep a journal or a log of how many times you miss an opportunity to react in a more elevated way. Write a brief note about why you reacted the way you did, and what you could've done better. Keep it simple and use it as a guide to track your progress. If you go thirty days without a setback great! If you're reverting back to your old ways once or twice a week, you know you'll have to take a look at other strategies that would be helpful to try.

Finally, as you know by now, I'm a big advocate of accountability. Find someone who you trust, and tell them what you're attempting to do. Let them know that you want to improve your level of emotional competence, and that you need their honest feedback and support as you work to accelerate that skill over the next sixty days.

Don't Fear

Working hard to adjust behaviors that you've had for many years. As you become more self aware, you'll be more and more open to embracing the lifelong challenge of becoming emotionally competent. As you begin, you may put too much pressure on yourself to be perfect. We all get flustered, we all get agitated and angry. Becoming emotionally competent is not about numbing our emotions; it's about being in control of how we display our emotions. Focus less on being perfect, and more on being present in each challenging situation. If you do this, you'll be far more successful in rebounding when you have a setback.

Personalize It

Now that we've discussed how you can improve your emotional competence, I want you to take a moment to complete the chart below; this is exactly what I asked you to do during the first thirty days of rebuilding your emotional competence. Try to complete this in one sitting so that you can really think deeply about how everything is interconnected.

My Unproductive Emotional Reactions	The Situations that Trigger these Reactions	My Triggers

PART TWO

INFLUENCE OTHERS

HANDLE CONFLICT
WITH EASE

*Leader-Ism #3: The Best Way To Prepare For Conflict
Is To Prepare For Conflict*

What 40 Screaming Girls Taught Me About Conflict

I know you'll never believe this, but yes, yours truly was the president of *Ladies of Elegance*, a travelling step team from my alma mater, Temple University. I was the president for two years and we won the most competitions during that time. I was in charge of creating the best entertainment experience for our audiences, and I was good at my job. We were the best non-Greek step team around, and it was thanks to my leadership abilities (wink). Oh, and if you're already lost about what a step team or "non-Greek" organization is, Google it and then come back to the chapter.

So, how did I transform the group from being known on campus to known around the entire region? What did I do to get forty young women to practice three days a week while working and going to school full time? How did I motivate them to be their best when we were on stage? The answer is simple: by yelling, bullying, and threatening to kick girls off the team if they didn't do what I said. That's right, sweet little Dr. Brandi was a jerk. In my defense, I didn't know I was a jerk because all of my jerkiness was working! We were winning, weren't we? We couldn't keep up with the amount of requests to perform in and around Philadelphia. You couldn't tell me I wasn't the perfect leader.

Outside of practice I was really cool with the girls, but in practice I was a drill sergeant. "Yo, you look a mess! Does that look right to you? Why are you looking so busted!?!" Oh man… it was bad. But I thought my angry motivation was exactly what the girls needed to step their game up. What I didn't realize was that while their performance skills were getting better on the outside, their self-esteem was being damaged on the inside.

So, we all know that what goes around comes around, right? I learned my lesson one day after drilling the girls for three hours. I handed out one insult too many and one girl had enough. She let me have it! I can't remember exactly what was said, but it included lots of eye-rolling, neck twisting, hand gestures, and expletives. After she was done, another girl added in *her* two cents, and then another. I was almost in tears by the time those girls let me have it. I'd pushed too hard, for too long, and it was time to give me a wakeup call.

By the end of the night, I'd gotten cursed out by more people than I'd like to admit. Over the next few weeks, I worked hard to repair as many relationships as I could. Not everyone was ready to forgive my evil ways, but what I realized was priceless. I was getting results by being a tyrant, so I had a false sense that my leadership approach was working. Rather than being collaborative or accommodating to the girls, I was rigid and took a "my way or the highway" approach. I trained them up to be the best performers, but I also lost their respect. And once the respect is gone, so is the influence. There was a point when they didn't listen to anything I had to say. All of our trophies and validation from the outside world wasn't worth the damaged relationships. As a leader, conflict is about managing the relationship first, and the issue second. Never forget that.

Sooner or later, you will encounter a conflict at work. It may be minor, it may be significant, but either way it's an opportunity that you need to prepare for. How you manage conflict as a leader should be different from how you managed it as a non-leader. Because you have power, you have to be even more purposeful and slightly strategic with how you handle conflict. The way you manage differences of opinions and competing agendas will determine how far your influence will ultimately reach.

Conflict is an opportunity for you to see the world through someone else's eyes. It's a time when you should be asking yourself, "Why are they seeing this issue in that way?" "What are they seeing that I'm not?" Your ability to develop a high level of conflict competence will accelerate your influence on the job.

What You Need to Know

Interpersonal conflict centers on two or more parties that have competing views, needs, or agendas. Conflict competence is all about using appropriate conflict management techniques in different situations. Most of us have a dominant conflict style and tend to use it for every conflict situation. For example, if you're an avoider, that means you don't like conflict and you rarely speak up to express your needs and wants.

Having the ability to change how you handle conflict in different situations is an essential tool to being an effective leader. In business, you'll encounter people with different levels of influence and power. You'll have to navigate high-stake and low-stake situations. You'll be dealing with people from different cultures and backgrounds. Your ability to maintain productive professional relationships relies in your ability to navigate conflict with agility and poise.

I'm not going to spend time summarizing and describing each of the conflict styles that exists. I strongly recommend that you do a quick Google search and find the Thomas-Kilman Conflict Styles Inventory. You can download the entire assessment for free and complete it when you have time. There are also supplemental readings that will provide you with a better understanding of the best and worst times to use a competitive, accommodating, collaborative, compromising, or avoiding approach. You'll learn so much about yourself by utilizing that assessment to benchmark where you are today.

Take Two

Two things to remember as you practice this leadership skill.

1. Stop Arguing

As a professional, having an argument with someone on the job should be something that you never experience. If you're an entrepreneur and you're running a business with your baby brother, you may have a spat. I'll let that slide. For everyone else, having a full blown argument at work is not an option. I understand that sometimes we have heated debates, but straight up arguing is unacceptable. If you're an arguer… quit cold turkey, today.

2. Stop Avoiding

As with arguing, we should not be allowed, as professionals, to avoid major issues at work. I'm not talking about trivial things, like who stole your yogurt from the refrigerator, or who didn't replace copy paper in the copy machine. That sort of stuff is irrelevant. I'm talking about real issues that are present at work. Playing nice or playing dumb, or playing scared won't cut it anymore. Once you have the tools to confront appropriately, put them to work and be brave enough to accept whatever comes next.

The Tough Stuff

Developing a strategic way of dealing with conflict is probably the toughest thing a leader can do. There are three challenges that you will face as you begin to develop your conflict competence. I'm going to outline each challenge so that you can prepare yourself to deal with it when it happens.

Getting Rid of Bad Habits

As with most of the new skills you will develop, the hardest part is getting rid of old habits. Shifting out of autopilot and making conscious decisions about how you will handle conflict is a muscle that you are going to have to build diligently and purposefully. Think about how conflict was handled in your household as a child. What did you observe? What were you implicitly and explicitly taught? What was acceptable? What are the dysfunctional habits that you've picked up along the way? Address these issues and then you'll be able to un-learn old bad habits that are keeping you from elevating your conflict competence.

Dealing With Difficult People

As you develop and refine your conflict management skills, it'll be tough to be on your best behavior when you encounter "difficult" people. These are the people who will rub you the wrong way, and leave a bad taste in your mouth. When this happens, your gut instinct will be to revert back to what you've always done. You may avoid the person like the plague. You may decide to give them a taste of their own medicine. When you feel the urge to succumb to your old habits, don't do it! Use that as an opportunity to confront with poise. We'll talk more about confrontation in a minute, but for now, all you need to do is get ready for the difficult people who will attempt to derail your progress.

Thriving in a Dysfunctional Organization

The worst place to practice building your conflict competence is in a dysfunctional organization. Why? Because chances are, there are very few models or processes for how to manage conflict effectively. If you're someone who works in a dysfunctional organization, be prepared to accelerate your skill building. You'll most likely encounter a conflict situation every day. Don't see this as a curse; see it as an awesome opportunity. In this case, consistency is key. Don't fall victim to your old habits, no matter what people are expecting you to do. You may get weird looks, odd questions, and push-back, but stay consistent and show people that you are making permanent changes to how you handle conflict. You don't have to *say* anything to anyone. Your actions will speak much louder than your words in this case. That means you don't have to announce that you're trying new things. Just demonstrate the new behavior and stay focused on handling conflict in a more productive manner.

The Secret to Success

The secret to success in building your conflict competence is learning how to adjust your conflict management style for different situations. When you encounter a conflict situation during a staff meeting, versus one-on-one with a colleague, your style should be different.

Remember, how you handle conflict should be in alignment with how you want to manage the relationship that you're in with each person. If you're invested in a long-term relationship with someone, you should be handling conflict in a way that will support the continued growth of that relationship. You should behave in a way that demonstrates that you still want to be in a mutually beneficial relationship in the future. Many times, we're harsh to those who are closest to us, or we drive ourselves crazy when someone who we barely know offends or disrespects us. If you're in conflict with someone who you're only interacting with once, why get offended when they step on your toes. If you find yourself in conflict with someone you don't need (i.e. you don't have an interdependent relationship), why choose to engage in a back-and-forth battle with them? The key to conflict competence is knowing how to react based on the relationship, and situation. To do that successfully, you'll have to be self-aware during conflict situations.

60-Day Implementation Plan

You are going to see amazing things happen for your leadership influence once you elevate your conflict competence. There are a few things you'll need to do in order to accelerate your growth in this area.

Day 1-30

The first and most important thing you need to do is identify your primary conflict style by completing the Thomas-Kilman Conflict Styles Inventory. Use online learning platforms like Udemy.com and Lynda.com to find courses on conflict management. This will give you a better sense of the various conflict styles and how your behavior falls within each category. You'll be able to identify some of your dysfunctional behaviors and become familiar with the theories and core tenets of conflict management. It'll serve you well, not only for your own conflict competence, but as you develop your employees.

Next, I want you to take a few weeks to observe the conflict styles of others. This is important because what you struggle with, others may not. You may notice that one of your colleagues is excellent at diffusing tense situations. If you're someone who gets frazzled during tense situations, observe what they do well and begin to incorporate their practices into your daily conflict management activities. Fill your gaps with what others do well.

Finally, during the first thirty days of implementing your new conflict management strategies, make a list of anticipated conflicts that you expect to encounter at work. Think about the last 90-days and conflicts that have happened in the immediate past. Reflect on the current state of your organization. What is the current climate like? What current projects, or market influences are impacting your organization? Those will also be clues that will help you identify and anticipate future conflicts that may arise. The best way to prepare for conflict is to prepare for conflict. Once you've identified potential conflicts, brainstorm a few productive ways you can manage the people and situations.

Day 31-60

I want you to confront any and all unresolved conflicts using your new conflict management techniques. The only way you'll get good at managing conflict is by working that new muscle as often as possible. One place to start is with the relationships you currently have. Maybe you and your siblings don't see eye-to-eye. Maybe you and your significant other are going through a rough patch. Maybe you don't get along with one of your coworkers or colleagues and it's straining your professional relationships. Whatever it is, make a decision today to confront it (head-first) within the next 60-days. If you don't think you can do it, just start the conversation off with, "My leadership advisor gave me an assignment..." Put it on me and go for it. Be open to the possibilities and don't look for a specific outcome. This is just practice to help build your skills.

Don't Fear

Get rid of the fear of confrontation. To confront just means to address someone; to acknowledge that an issue is present. Your fear will diminish as you develop productive ways to confront others. I personally use two strategies when it comes to confronting others. My first strategy is best used when you're speaking to someone and they say something that you perceive as being inappropriate, disrespectful, or unprofessional. You simply ask, "Excuse me?" This will prompt the other person to quickly reflect on what they just said. Smart people will most likely rephrase what they said, or apologize before the conflict escalates. For others, it may go over their head, and for that, I have my back-up technique, which is called perception checking. I didn't create this process, but I've used it for years to facilitate productive confrontations.

Perception checking is a three step process. The first step requires you to state to another person the *facts* about a troubling behavior that you've observed. Don't add any additional details, and don't 'color' your statement with extra words, a rude tone, or an eye-roll. Keep your composure and just stick to the facts.

Next, provide two interpretations that could explain why the person said or did what they did. One of your interpretations should be something that will let them off the hook. The other should be exactly what you think they meant. The truth is: neither of the interpretations that you present may be valid to them. That's fine, because the last step is asking them point-blank, "Can you clarify what you meant by that statement?" This gives them an opportunity to explain themselves. Be patient, bold, and ready to positively react to what they say. It'll be awkward for sure, but it creates a space for that other person to own their poor behavior. This is an opportunity for you find a way to maintain your dignity as you address the poor behavior of others around you. It's a powerful tool to use and it'll help you get over the fear of confronting others. There are many resources online about perception checking. Check them out!

Personalize It

In this section, I want you to take some time to write out some of the fears you have that are associated with confrontation and conflict. Acknowledging these fears are essential to your growth as a leader. Reflect on what you write and even spark a discussion with your accountability partner or someone you trust. You may check their perception about how they've observed you during conflict situations. For the purposes of this activity, think about both your personal and professional experiences and how they've contributed to some of the fears you have.

Fear Around Conflict & Confrontation	Where did this fear come from?	How has/will this fear impact your leadership influence?

4

BECOME A MASTER COMMUNICATOR

Leader-Ism #4: Your Words Have Power.
Choose Them Wisely.

What My 3-year Old Taught Me about Communication

Remember the show, *Kids Say the Darndest Things*? I used to love that show, and after my daughter was born, I had a front row seat to my own "kids say the darndest" right at home. I remember that 3-year old phase. Some think about the "terrible twos". In my opinion the fun doesn't start until they hit three. During this stage, my daughter Zuri was testing the limits of everything and loving every minute of it. Unfortunately, I didn't love it nearly as much. I was a busy working mom, graduate student, and entrepreneur. I was low on patience and pretty uptight most of the time. The stress of life impacted our relationship and I wasn't much fun to be around.

I will never forget one day that I picked my daughter up from daycare with less than a minute to spare. I was that frantic mom who would show up one minute before daycare closed. My tires would screech as I turned into the parking lot. I'd speed over the speed bumps, jump out of the car, and run across the parking lot like I was a criminal being chased by the cops. As I got close to her classroom my sprint would turn into a brisk walk. I'd attempt to appear calm and say, "Hi sweetie, ready to go?" The young girls who worked there would roll their eyes in disgust. I was the only thing stopping them from clocking out and going home.

I'd give my daughter a quick hug, put her coat on and drag her to the car in a hurry, "c'mon sweetie, walk faster." As we drove home on this day, I didn't turn any music on, I didn't ask Zuri how her day was, and I didn't say one word. I was tired and I needed silence. I had a horrible day.

When we got home, I put her in the bathtub for a quick wash-up. When I was done, I took her to the living room to play while I prepped dinner in the kitchen. After about five or six minutes, I heard a huge crash coming from the living room. My heart skipped a beat and the first thing that ran through my mind was, "My baby!" As I turned around, I caught a glimpse of a huge vase shattered into pieces on the floor. It had fallen off of my book case. My daughter was standing there with a stunned look on her face. She had that Steve Urkel, "Did I do that?" look. I made eye contact with her and began to yell, "No, no, no, no, no!" I stomped across the wooden floors, stopped right in front of her, knelt down, and yelled, "that's a no no!" in the most evil voice you could imagine. That was the straw that broke my back that night. Mommy had enough.

Before I could continue, she wrapped her arms around herself and cried out, "Ouch, mommy, that hurts." I saw the look on her face, her bottom lip started to quiver; tears were welling up in her eyes, her head tilted slowly toward the floor. And then the cry started. You know that cry that kids do that starts off silent and then turns into a scream? Yea, that cry. I was caught off guard by her response. She said "ouch" as if I hit her, but I didn't. To her, my words "hit" her. My words assaulted her. I had hurt my baby girl's feelings and I was devastated. At that moment, I realized the power of communication. It can be used to build up, or tear down important personal and professional relationships.

Communication is the most important skill to master as a new leader. How you communicate reflects your values, your level of self-esteem, and your level of confidence. When you communicate, you can't hide the truth about who you are and what you believe about yourself and others. How you communicate will determine who shows you respect, offers you opportunities, and provides you with access to their influential friends and business partners. How you communicate will determine how fast you're able to spark change within your organization and how well you're able to convince potential clients to purchase your products or services. Your ability to demonstrate power and poise through the use of verbal and nonverbal communication will be the driver for you leadership success.

What You Need to Know

Masterful communication requires that you first become aware of your communication rules and the things that you believe are acceptable and unacceptable when it comes to communication. Our communication rules are embedded within our culture. So for example, some cultures may follow rules like, "closed mouths don't get fed," or the idea that if you want something you better open your mouth and make a request to get it. Other cultures may value the rule that "it's better to be seen and not heard," or the idea that it's better to do less talking in public and private contexts. It's important to note that communication rules are different for different cultures. Some of the communication rules and norms that you have accepted may not be useful in your workplace and in the world of business. This is why developing leadership communication skills are important to your overall success.

How you communicate is an extension of your leadership brand. It's the primary method that you use to present your brand to others. The great thing about communication is that it's 100% controlled by you! You can easily adjust your communication style to fit the needs of your position. Many leaders fail simply due to poor communication. Rather than changing their communication style, they just chalk it up to, "That's how I am." Communication, when used strategically, can influence others in a powerful way.

Every communication interaction either builds up or tears down a relationship. Think about your current relationships. I'm sure you'll realize that you have positive communication interactions with the people who you have thriving relationships with. On the flip side, you probably don't have the best communication with the people who you don't get along with. Miscommunication is usually the reason why personal and professional relationships fail. I always tell my clients, if they want to repair broken relationships, they must first change the way they communicate with that person. It's quite simple when you think about it.

There's a concept called relational communication that was developed by psychologists and communication scholars years ago. One thing that I love about this concept is that it helps us understand how important our communication is to our interpersonal relationships. There are two concepts within this framework that are my favorite. One is called confirmation, and the other is called disconfirmation. In a nutshell, confirmation is when you communicate with someone in a way that says "you have value". Disconfirmation is when you communicate with someone in a way that says "you don't have value".

For example, when you say hello to someone and they ignore you, they're nonverbally saying "I don't value you". When you share your feelings with someone and they abruptly change the subject, they are saying, "I don't value what you have to say, therefore, I don't value you." The opposite is true with confirming communication. When you confirm someone you're affirming their identity and showing that they have value.

My challenge for you as a leader is to confirm as many people as consistently as possible. Make people feel that they are valued by you. Relational communication is so awesome because it's all about the meaning *behind* the verbal and nonverbal messages that we send and receive during interpersonal interactions. Remember the saying, "it's not what you say, it's how you say it?" That's what this is all about.

As a leader, be purposeful about how you speak to others and the meaning they may derive from those interactions. Like they say, "people will always remember how you made them feel when they were around you."

Take Two

Two things to remember as you practice this leadership skill.

1. Ask More Questions

Questions are a great way to improve your communication skills. Ask more questions during conversations, in meetings, and when you meet new people. Asking questions is less about the questions you ask and more about developing a knack for questioning the status quo. When most people think about communication, they think about how much they talk or how well they speak. When it comes to leadership, all of those things matter, but what's just as important is your ability to use communication to challenge the thinking of others around you. Asking thoughtful questions is a good start.

2. Listen and Be Present

Listening is an important communication skill that often gets overlooked. Listening is just as important as speaking. When it comes to listening, I want you to be present in meetings and in conversations. The number one thing I want you to do is stop thinking about your next statement when other people are talking. We all do it, but it hinders our ability to actively listen during conversations. As you develop your communication skills don't forget about improving your listening skills as well.

The Tough Stuff

To control how others perceive you, and especially to influence and persuade others, master positive relational communication. As easy as it may sound, there are some challenges to consider when elevating this aspect of your communication style.

Being Authentic and Not Perfect

Authenticity is central to becoming a masterful communicator. Don't get authenticity confused with perfection. As a leader, you will make communication mistakes. The goal is not for you to be perfect; it's for you to be authentic. I can't stand to be around professionals (usually corporate folk) who all speak in the same way. They use the same jargon, same tone, same everything. It reminds me of news reporters. I wonder if they all took a class on how to talk like reporter robots. For you, make sure to focus on authentic communication, not perfect communication. Perfect communication is when everyone in a meeting smiles, nods, and agrees just because it's the status quo. Authentic communication is respectfully presenting an alternative perspective and speaking up when it matters the most.

Tailoring Your Communication for the Relationship

It's important that you begin to tailor your communication style based on the types of relationships you have. With some people, you may have to be more direct. With other people, you may have to be more indirect. When giving feedback to a colleague you've known for a while, you may be able to use "tough love." On the other hand, if you're giving feedback to a new employee, you may choose to stick to the facts and take a more analytical approach. When you begin to accommodate others by making subtle changes to your communication style, you're able to have a greater influence on the relationship and the person. You know what they say, "appeal to your audience." The same is true with interpersonal communication.

The Secret to Success

To successfully elevate your communication, you must change the mindsets that are connected to your dysfunctional patterns of communication. You'll slip back into old habits if you don't ask yourself questions about the communication rules that are no longer serving you. Questions like, who told me that it was alright to cut others off in the middle of their sentences just to get my point across? Who told me that it was okay to shut down and refuse to respond to someone just because I don't like what they're saying? Who told me that people will think you're conceited if you communicate with confidence? Who said that my southern accent would make people think I was less intelligent?

I could provide example after example of dysfunctional values that negatively impact our ability to communicate with power and poise. Confronting your dysfunctional beliefs around communication is 100% necessary for you to master communication as a new and influential leader.

60-Day Implementation Plan

It takes time to remove your ingrained patterns of communication. It also takes focus and determination. That's why I want to present you with three specific things you can do to build your communication competence in the next sixty days.

Identify Your Poor Communication Patterns

The first thing you need to do is to create a list of all of your ugly, weak, and ineffective communication practices. In what ways do you communicate with others that aren't in alignment with the leadership brand you want to portray? What things do you say that turn people off? What words do you use that make others perceive you as weak or lacking confidence? What things do you do that send the message "you are not valued" to others? Write those things down and begin to reflect on how you can make immediate improvements.

Ask for Feedback from Others

Solicit feedback from your closest family, friends, and trusted colleagues. Simply ask a few people to share their candid opinion regarding your communication style. Take what they say with a grain of salt, but add it to your development list and see how it compares to your self-assessment.

Create Communication Goals

Once you have a comprehensive list of dysfunctional patterns of communication, create a separate list of goals for improving your communication. This can be done in lots of different ways, but I like to attach each behavior to a person, and attach the goal to both that person and behavior. Here's why: communication is interpersonal and between you and other specific people. Rather than coming up with general goals, being specific and saying "I will not interrupt X coworker during staff meetings" will accelerate your change in behavior. The more specific you are, the easier it'll be to transform your behaviors.

Don't Fear

As your communication changes, your relationships with important others will change. Don't fear other's reactions to your new communication approach. Maybe you're speaking up for yourself now. Maybe you're creating boundaries by saying "no" a lot more. Maybe you're giving people direct feedback instead of indirectly suggesting things.

Initially, some people may not know how to react to you. They may feel threatened by the changes you are making, and that's okay. Be ready for it and be ready to ignore any negative reactions you may receive.

Personalize It

In this section, I want you to think about all of the people who you admire, who have masterful communication skills. Identify what you like about their communication style and start to brainstorm ways that you can incorporate some of their practices into your daily communication practices.

Person I Admire	Their Communication Style	Why I like it so much.

PART THREE

THREE

GET RESULTS

5

GET READY FOR
ORGANIZATIONAL POLITICS

Leader-Ism #5: If You Can't Beat Them, Join Them

What My PhD Experience Taught Me about Politics

I could write an entire book about my PhD experience and all of the ups and downs that I experienced as I pursued my doctoral degree. I remember reaching my fifth year in the program. I'd been working around the clock to finish my manuscript. Over the years, I missed birthday parties, family outings, and holiday gatherings, all because I was working on completing my degree. There were times when I wouldn't see my children for days at a time. My life was consumed with writing, editing, and researching. By the fifth year I knew that I was almost done, so I stayed the course, remained optimistic and continued to hammer away at my manuscript. All I needed was final approval from my dissertation chair to go to the next phase of the process.

For those who aren't aware, your dissertation chair is the person who works closely with you on your research. Essentially, they help you get to the finish line. Unfortunately, my chair was MIA most of the time. She rarely returned my phone calls, and her email response time was three to four weeks at best. In the beginning we had a great working relationship, but as the years went by, she became less and less available.

I had reached my wits end at the end of that fifth year. I was itching to graduate and I was stuck waiting around for that phone call for way too long. In true Brandi fashion, I jumped into problem-solving mode. I spent two full weeks talking to other professors, asking them what I should do. To my surprise, I found out that I could replace my chair by completing a simple form in the graduate school. Why didn't I think of that a while ago?

I decided to call the graduate school to let them know my plans, and I got the "okay" from one of the directors. I filled out the paperwork, turned it in, and got a new committee chair. It was as easy as 1-2-3 and I was excited at the thought of finally getting back on track towards graduation.

I sent a farewell email to my former chair and never looked back. I worked on editing my manuscript all Summer and *one week* before the start of the semester I got an email with a subject like that read, "I Need Closure About Your Decision" from my former dissertation chair. What?!?! Where had she been? I sent that farewell email almost three months prior and got no response! All of a sudden, she needs closure?

My heart fluttered as I opened the email. I was scared to see what she had written. I read through the email carefully, and between me and you, let's just say it was a not-so-nice email telling me how much I suck. She demanded an apology and said that she would be taking matters into her own hands regarding my decision. I didn't bother to respond as I thought I was untouchable since she was no longer on my committee. I archived the message and didn't think about it again... until I got a call from the graduate school.

Long story short, she went on an all out campaign to get me back for removing her as my chair. On one occasion, she cornered my new chair in the hallway and played a not so fun game of twenty-one questions asking why he agreed to come aboard as my chair. The head of the graduate school brought me in for an "off the record" meeting to give me a verbal butt-whipping. I was told by him that I was "burning bridges" and that I'd "never get a recommendation for a job" if I didn't agree to write an apology letter to my former chair. He even agreed to pay for a semester of my tuition if I wrote an apology letter. I was like, "did I just get bribed?" Suddenly the professors who I'd developed relationships with avoided me like the plague. I was told by one professor that my former chair was a "bully" but that no one wanted to deal with her nasty attitude. So, I had no shield of protection. I wrote letters to the college ombudsperson, the dean of the department, and not one person gave me the courtesy of a response. I was a student in need of guidance with how to deal with a disgruntled former chair, and no one cared.

I soon learned that although there *was* a form to replace dissertation chairs, **NO ONE EVER USED IT**! Most students who had problems with their dissertation chair just sucked it up. Everyone knew that that was the "rule"; everyone except me. I soon realized that there were certain rules of engagement. Unsaid rules that were always in-play. I guess I didn't get the memo that time. But I understand now, the power of organizational politics and how they can ruin your professional experience.

Organizational politics is never about what's right or wrong. Organizational politics are about what's acceptable and unacceptable within a particular organization. In my case, it was totally acceptable for a professor to take months to respond back to a student. It was completely unacceptable, however, for students to replace their chairs because of it. There were norms that I wasn't aware of, and I learned the hard way that a strategic approach is necessary to thriving in highly political organizations.

Every company has some degree of organizational politics; those invisible rules about who has social, formal, and informal power. I'd like to think of organizational politics as a game that every leader must play. There's no way to exist outside of organizational politics if you want to thrive as a leader. Effective leaders are able to navigate organizational politics with ease. That doesn't mean they *like* the bureaucracy, but they acknowledge it, and devise a plan to be successful in spite of it.

What You Need to Know

Leaders who fight against the organizational machine are often pushed out in formal (getting fired) or informal ways (being alienated). You never want to stick out like a sore thumb, especially when you're new. As soon as you see the first red flag that lets you know that the company you're working for doesn't have it together, start making a game plan to succeed within the structure that is already there.

Voicing your opinion about the company politics is a waste of time. Believe me; everyone else at your company knows that there are company politics at play. They don't need you to validate it. Instead of focusing on whether there's an absence or presence of company politics, shift your attention to studying who the key players are and how you can survive within the organizational ecosystem.

I'm not an expert on organizational politics, but I've worked in some pretty dysfunctional places. Here are a few key things to observe within your organization. First, identify the people who have power based on their title versus those who have power based on other social factors (i.e. seniority, tenure, being related to the CEO etc.). You may realize that one of the key executives has no real power, because the other two executives make all of the final decisions. You may notice that employees who have been there for ten or more years have more influence than newer employees. You may realize that the leadership makes decisions, not based on actual data, but based on how they feel. There are hundreds of examples of organizational politics that we can reference. You don't need to know all of them. You just need to discover what's going on within *your* organization.

Once you've identified the key players who have power, you can make calculated decisions about ways in which you will not contribute to the dysfunctional bureaucracy that's already there.

Take Two

Two things to remember as you practice this leadership skill.

1. Observe, Observe, Observe

When you're in a new social setting, observation is key. Take some time to observe how others are interacting. Who has the most social clout? What are the appropriate and accepted behaviors during meetings? Being a fly on the wall is the perfect way to gather information about how to behave appropriately in new social contexts.

2. Become a Double Agent

Some highly dysfunctional organizations can be tough for new leaders. I've found that it's easier to deal with organizational politics if you become what I call, a "double agent". When you walk in the door each morning you have to become a "different" person. You can't bring your authentic self into these environments. When you're a double agent, you're there on assignment. You're on a mission and it may require you to change some aspects of your personality or leadership style to survive. By creating this alter ego, you can detach yourself from the dysfunctions within your organization. Think of it as going undercover.

The Tough Stuff

It's frustrating to work within a dysfunctional and highly political work environment. It sucks the life out of you, and sometimes it stops you from being your best self. Your goal in managing organizational politics is to strengthen your ability to *adapt* to all of the "crazy" that's happening around you. You can be *in* the crazy and not *of* the crazy, if you know what I mean. That's *exactly* where you need to be.

There are two challenges that you'll encounter as you learn how to manage the politics within your organization.

Not Getting Sucked into the Drama

It'll be challenging to navigate politics without becoming a part of the drama and dysfunction. Often times, those of us who are discouraged with company politics unintentionally become a part of the problem by becoming disgruntled, angry, or disengaged. We become so "anti-establishment", that our own toxic behaviors creep into our daily routines. How we communicate, and how we handle conflict becomes affected because we succumb to the drama and discord that is present within our organizations. Don't add to the drama; focus on getting results so that you can either gain more power within your organization, or leave and go to another more "functional" company.

Not Getting Frustrated

No one likes to go to work every day just to be met with haters, drama, politics, lies, and negative energy. It's a harsh reality that you may have to face as a leader. Don't get frustrated to the point that it has a negative effect on your work or reputation. Don't start slacking off. If you are frustrated, don't let it show. The best leaders aren't effective because they're in non-political environments. They're successful because they learn how to thrive within dysfunctional organizations. It'll take time, lots of energy, and maybe some therapy, but it can be done! It's naive to think that you're going to leave and find another company with a better culture. Every organization has its own quirks. Focus less on what's out of your control and focus more on what's *in* your control.

The Secret to Success

The secret to being successful at managing organizational politics is, staying true to your core values. No matter how horrible your workplace is, don't let the negativity rub off on you. No matter how political your organization is, don't compromise who you are and what you stand for to fit in. All you have in the business world is your integrity and reputation. If you're working in an organization that lies to its customers, takes advantage of its employees or engages in unethical business practices, make a plan to speak up for what's right. The next time you overhear a coworker being disrespectful to someone, step in and let them know that their behavior is unacceptable. When you witness an argument happening in a staff meeting, speak up and challenge your colleagues to communicate in a more dignified way.

Weak leaders are a waste of space. Too many organizations are where they are today, because of weak leaders who turn a blind eye to injustices happening all around them. If you're ready to be a leader, be ready for both the good and the bad. It comes with the territory. Stay true to who you are, and be willing to take a stand when it matters the most.

60-Day Implementation Plan

As a new leader, it's important that you do some specific things during the first sixty days on the job.

Day 1-30

During your first month on the job, take some time to observe the norms of your company. Observe group dynamics to get information about how everyone relates to one another. Once you do that, identify the glaring dysfunctions that just don't make sense. Who has the real power? Who makes and influences major decisions? Who has the most "fan club" members (i.e. workplace friends that will never tell them that they did anything wrong)? Take the time to conduct a thorough (informal) assessment of your organization's culture.

Day 31-60

For the next thirty days, start building your dream team. Find other people at various levels within the organization to develop professional relationships with. Think of these as important allies who will help forward your leadership agenda. Some people may be mentors, others may be fan club members, and still others may be go-getters and high achievers. You'll need to call on these important others when the going gets tough.

They will inform you, shield you, and support you during challenging times. Be careful with this though. My focus is not on quantity, it's on quality. Be discerning about who you recruit for your dream team. Ideally, it should take you about 90-days to build relationships with your dream team. If you look out for them, they'll look out for you.

Don't Fear

This may seem obvious, but don't fear the organizational machine. If you work in a really dysfunctional company, you may be on edge every single day. You may feel like there's a target on your back. You may silence your voice for fear of rubbing others the wrong way, or being "found out" as someone who doesn't agree with the organizational politics. Whatever you do, don't become an enslaved, paranoid, fearful leader who relinquishes his/her voice and power because of company politics. Would you rather suck it up to keep your job, while being miserable and useless, or would you rather find ways to navigate the drama, while making plans to jump ship and find a better opportunity? I suggest the latter.

Personalize It

In this section, I want you to write down some personal reflections about our discussion on organizational politics. New leaders often fail because of their idealistic and overly optimistic vision for how companies operate. This exercise will help you acknowledge your personal perspectives regarding organizational politics.

When I think about organizational politics, it makes me feel....

When I think about standing up in subtle ways to address injustices within my organization, I feel.....

6

GET READY TO PUT IN WORK

Leader-Ism #6: What Got You Here,
Won't Keep You Here

What Being an Entrepreneur Has Taught Me About Putting in Work

Being an entrepreneur is hard work. I mean really hard work. Going to work and having a guaranteed paycheck is *much* easier. I thought I had an excellent work ethic, until I made the choice to become an entrepreneur. What made me successful as a career professional and as a student didn't do much for me as an entrepreneur.

When you're working in corporate America, you may think twelve-hour days are a lot; but when you work for yourself, you work for twelve *days* at a time. The grind and the hustle is real. In the beginning, I didn't get paid for every day that I worked. Entrepreneurship is all about seasons of growth and development. During some seasons, you need to be planting seeds, and during other seasons you need to be fertilizing the soil. The work that it takes to get to the "harvest" season is incredible. Most people can't hack it. Not because it's hard, but because it's unpredictable. It doesn't matter how much you plan or how hard you work, there's no hard science to predicting how much success you'll have as an entrepreneur. Business takes some significant trial and error before you get it right. The bottom line is: you have to be willing to **put in work** to see the fruits of your labor. There's no easy way around it. Work, not luck, will account for most of your future success.

What You Need to Know

The things that make entrepreneurs successful can also help new leaders get amazing results on the job. As you read the rest of this chapter, think about what you can do to think and act more like an entrepreneur every day.

As a new leader, it's easy to get caught up in wanting to make a huge difference as soon as you arrive. I get it; you have something to prove. You've gone through the five-step interview process, salary negotiations, and training, and now you want to prove that you deserve to be there. My advice to you? Pace yourself. Getting results as a leader is not about how fast you can make your mark. It's about sustaining results long enough to have a long-term impact. Most new leaders don't make it past their first year. You need to be laser focused on getting acclimated to the company culture, and making a strategic plan for change. No matter how much pressure you're receiving from the "higher-ups." Don't burn out too quickly. Remember one simple phrase: endure to the end.

Your number one job as a new leader is simple: put in work! There are no short cuts, no fast-track options, and no one who will do the work for you. In order to earn your stripes as a leader, you're going to have to put *yourself* through leadership boot-camp. Rather than thinking that you've "arrived", understand that you are starting from scratch. You are on a new professional level, and you have to master the level you're on before getting the next promotion. Your job is not to rush up the corporate ladder; it's to become so good at your job that people will pull you up to the next rung on that ladder.

It should take you at least one year to get the "kinks" out of your leadership approach. You'll have to constantly adjust and adapt to the new environment, the new role, the new people, and the organizational politics. During your first year in leadership, you're going to miss the mark a few times. And honestly, if you're not missing the mark and failing every once in a while, that means you're playing too small. It means you're operating too much by the book. More importantly, it means you're missing learning opportunities. Think about it: why play it safe and "win" at everything you do, and miss out on opportunities to stretch yourself? A good challenge will show you what you're made of. Don't hide behind trying to be perfect. Be strategic, but put some solid effort into trying new things and developing your leadership skills. Remember, what got you to this level won't keep you there.

Take Two

Two things to remember as you practice this leadership skill.

1. Stay Focused on Your Core Leadership Activities

Entrepreneurs have "core money making activities". Those are things they must do every day to make money for their businesses. As a leader, you have to make sure that you're working, thinking, and behaving like a leader. That means that you need to build the habit of becoming laser-focused on doing the things that will elevate your leadership and your organization. Don't get caught up in micromanaging others or the paperwork associated with your job. Don't spend too much time "on the floor" with your team if your expertise yields better results in another area. Identify your *core leadership activities* and use them to drive success for your company.

2. Do Something Scary Once a Month

I keep myself "on my toes" by finding something scary to do once a month. At the beginning of each year I make a list of twelve activities that will challenge me in different ways. Some of them are business challenges, others are fun challenges, like taking a flying trapeze course (I'm afraid of heights), or learning ballroom salsa (I can do a mean running man, but ballroom salsa is not exactly in my wheelhouse). Every time you push yourself outside of your comfort zone, you strengthen your ability to *thrive* outside of your comfort zone. You also prove to yourself that you can accomplish "scary" things. This translates well in business and will help you take chances as a leader.

The Tough Stuff

It's easy for me to tell you that you need to simply put in work, but it's not that easy, and I get that. There are two areas that I want you to focus on as you embark on your leadership journey: **not keeping score, and not doing it all by yourself.**

Not Keeping Score

As a new leader, you want to make sure that you're contributing, that you're showing others that you deserve a seat at the leadership table. Remember not to get caught up in keeping score. Many leaders fall into the trap of doing a self assessment every day. They're keeping track of everything that went right and everything that went horribly wrong.

I'm an advocate for self-reflection, but there's a fine line that I don't want you to cross. Instead of keeping score daily, reflect on your monthly performance. Don't get frustrated if you have a bad month or two. That's fine. That shows that you have lots to work on. Don't be too hard on yourself during that process of assessing your own performance.

Not Doing It All By Yourself

You're the leader, but you can't achieve success by yourself. You will need others to help forward your agenda. Others who desperately want to help you may build resentment because you're not including them in the work. You're not giving them an opportunity to earn their stripes and contribute as an emerging leader.

During your first year, identify people who can help you get your job done. Don't look for perfection. You may find a few people who need development and guidance, and that's okay. Train and develop them and then throw them to the wolves. Just kidding. Give them small responsibilities, then larger responsibilities so that they can strengthen their performance over time. Make a conscious effort to include others in your plans for change within your organization.

The Secret to Success

The secret to success for *putting in work* is having a plan. If you're a current or aspiring leader, you most likely have a great work ethic. You're no stranger to hard work. Just make sure you're not on your own personal hamster wheel going around and around without actually making progress. Working hard, putting in long hours, and being on your grind *is* admirable. That's what leaders are paid to do; to go above and beyond. But make sure you have an action plan that will keep you focused on the *outcomes* you're trying to achieve. If you don't make progress, you won't get results. It's just that simple. There are lots of leaders putting in twelve-hour days who aren't making progress within their organizations. It's a waste of time and energy. Identify your goals, make a plan, and put in work! That's a simple recipe for leadership success.

60-Day Implementation Plan

For your first sixty days on the job, I need you to slowly turn the dial up on your work habits. Start off slow and then over time accelerate your pace and plan for change. Here are some specific things you need to do right out of the gate to accelerate your potential for results.

Day 1-30

During the first thirty days, you need to learn the basics of your position. What are the daily activities you need to master to be successful at your job? You need to learn important processes, technology, and systems. Don't add your own "flavor" during the first thirty days. Just follow your job description and any advice you can get from your colleagues. Once you feel like you have a basic understanding of what your role requires, conduct your own on-the-job qualitative research. Take time to understand other positions and how they work in conjunction with yours. Get a grip on who does what and how important each of their roles is to making the organization function.

Day 31-60

For the next thirty days, I want you to get in gear and put in work. Now that you know what to do, do it to the best of your ability and start to perform at a higher level. Push yourself far outside of your comfort zone and strive to become a top performer. During this time, create a plan for how to overcome the challenging aspects of your position.

If you have lots of paperwork to do and it piles up every week, make a plan to become more efficient. If your job is meeting-heavy, think about consolidating your meetings on certain days. Month one is about immersing yourself in your new position. Month two is about making the role your own. It's about creating your own unique systems and methods to become a top performer on the job.

Don't Fear

When you're promoted to a new position, you're excited, nervous, and thrilled at starting a new chapter in your professional life. Don't worry about making mistakes. That's a part of being a leader. As long as you're not lying, cheating, or engaging in some other unethical behavior, you'll survive. If you get too caught up in not making mistakes, you'll become ineffective and stifle your own growth and development.

Personalize It

In this section, I want you to reflect on any apprehensions or fears you have as you start your new leadership position. What are you most nervous about? What challenges are you anticipating? In what areas do you want to develop?

I am nervous about...	I am anticipating these challenges	In my new position, I want to learn...

IMPLEMENTATION GUIDE

Branding Kickstart
Emotional Competence
Conflict Competence
Communication Skills
Overcoming Politics
How To "Put In Work"
*Bonus-Networking

SECTION 1
IMPLEMENTATION GUIDE

BRANDING KICKSTART

Designing your professional brand doesn't have to be complicated. Here are a few questions that will help you begin to identify who you are as a leader. Take your time answering each question and walking through each activity to begin the process of developing your professional brand.

How You Are Perceived vs. How You Want to be Perceived

1. Identify 3-5 phrases that others would use to describe you as a professional. Think about your peers, supervisors, supervisees, allies, and even people who you don't have a strong rapport with. What phrases would they use to describe you today?

1.

_____

2.

_____

3.

_____

4.

_____

5.

_____

2. Now, identify 3-5 words that you *want* to be associated with your professional leadership brand. Be authentic, honest, and realistic about your selection. This exercise is less about creating a superhuman leadership brand, and more about you being practical about your strengths and how they can be used to help you gain respect, influence others, and get results.

1.

_____

2.

_____

3.

_____

4.

5.

List of Leadership Traits

If you're having a tough time selecting your leadership traits, it may be helpful to look at this select list below. Scan the full list and circle each of the phrases that are true to who you are as a leader and professional. Then, narrow down your selection to the top 3-5 that are the most relevant to your industry and current or aspiring role.

Physical
- High energy level
- Physical stamina
- Tolerance for stress
- Not concerned about being overworked
- Vitality

Social
- Well-adjusted
- Oriented toward improving self, not denying weaknesses
- Behavior is consistent with values espoused
- Detached: can treat followers in a fair, objective fashion
- Honest, ethical, trustworthy: promises kept, fulfills responsibility

- Able to convert purpose and vision to action, and produce results
- Behavioral flexibility: adjust behavior to fit the situation
- "Make people feel that they are at the very heart of things and that, when they are, they are making contributions to the success of the organization."
- Understands others, knows how to influence them
- Empathy, social insight, charm, tact, diplomacy, persuasiveness
- Bases decisions on reality and needs of others, not self-interest
- Listens, empowers others, generates trust, negotiates collaboratively, resolves conflicts
- Strong motivator
- Superior listener
- Understands small group dynamics
- Emphasizes partnership
- Monitors and helps followers get work done well
- Persuades others to follow, not rely on authority to get things done.
- Cooperates and collaborates with others
- Ability to influence others
- Finds common ground with all types of people and builds rapport with them
- Takes initiative in social situations
- Appraises readiness/resistance of followers to move in a particular direction, senses when there is dissent or confusion

Intellectual/Intelligence

- Learns from experience and adapts to change
- Possess extensive knowledge used by subordinates to perform the work
- Develops inspirational image of new product or service
- Good judgment, foresight, intuition, creativity
- Ability to find meaning and order in ambiguous, uncertain events
- Self-knowledge
- Effectively plans, organizes and solves problems
- Coordinates separate specialized parts of organization
- Understands how external events will affect organization
- Honest attitude towards facts, objective truth
- Decisive: get the facts, assess information, and act, even if all information is not available, or others are not happy with decision
- Asks for more responsibility
- Knows how to delegate
- "Willingness to ask questions and to search openly and without bias for practical answers to the most vexing problems."
- "Learned to experiment and withhold judgment until they have objectively assessed a situation and identified a well-reasoned course of action."
- Plans how to deal with criticism by listing benefits of project in advance and prepares to articulate them to others

- Willing to ignore conventional wisdom in terms of looking at a problem and trying to strike out in a different direction.
- Knowledge of organization and how it operates
- Anticipates how others will react to situations and prepares to minimize the impact
- Doesn't react right away, stands back and considers the situation, suspends judgment until facts are in
- Eager to explore new approaches to work
- Able to combine both hard and questionable data and intuitive guesses to arrive at a conclusion
- Bases decisions and strategies on sound intuitive and rational judgments and accurate appraisal of the potentialities of coworkers and opponents

Communication

- Ability to communicate
- Ability to articulate a vision and persuade others
- Have and communicate purpose, direction, and meaning
- Have clear goals and are determined to achieve them
- Communicates passion to others
- Good communication skills are essential for a leader to get followers aligned behind the overarching goals of the organization.
- Use metaphors that others can relate to in order to symbolize their vision and inspire others

- Experts at one-to-one communication
- Superior speakers – major advantage, not true of all leaders
- Excellent writing skills
- Creates and maintains a communications network
- Has people keep them informed on problem situations
- Networks with people inside the organization (including those at the bottom of the hierarchy)
- Maintains contacts outside the organization and profession that may have certain knowledge and different viewpoints from those within
- Doesn't depend on only one source for information
- Able to communicate with key individuals in "areas of specialization that may each have a different dialect"

Emotional

- Self-Confidence: may be more likely to attempt to influence, to attempt more challenging tasks
- Desire to improve, understand own strengths and weaknesses, self-objectivity
- Emotional intelligence: the extent to which a person is attuned to his or her own feelings and the feelings of others
- Self-awareness, empathy, self-regulation
- Not dwell on mistakes, view as opportunities to learn and move on
- Ambitious

- Courage, not paralyzed by fear of failure
- Knows self: deep understanding of one's emotions, strengths, weaknesses, needs, and drives
- Loves what he/she does; loves doing it
- Risk takers, confident to take risks, handle negative reactions to outcome
- Not intimidated by superiors
- Personal competence
- Believe they have control over own destinies
- Optimistic
- Accept responsibility
- Persistent: does not let potential objections or criticisms stop him or her; despite resistance or setbacks, keeps going and stays the course.
- Exhibits concern for others, shows genuine interest, gives "personal touch," gives others recognition for success
- Encourages and engages opposing viewpoints and ideas, not threatened by them
- Perceived by others as constant and reliable: picks position or idea and sticks to it
- Self-disciplined in developing important skills
- Determination
- Good at managing one's emotions

Trustworthy

- Caring – genuinely concerned with followers' lives and well-being
- Empathize and care about implications of actions
- Constancy – staff believe leader will support them, defend them and come through for them

Actions Related to Each Leadership Trait

If you found it difficult to narrow down your leadership traits, don't worry. Of course you have more than five leadership strengths! I am challenging you to narrow down your selection so that you can begin to create a focused brand for yourself. You'll understand more after completing the exercise in this next section.

Now that you've narrowed down your leadership traits, take a moment to identify key daily actions that are in alignment with each of your selected traits. The goal here is for you to be crystal clear about your brand and the things you'll need to do day in and day out for your colleagues and team to begin perceiving you in the way that you intend. Others will begin to adapt their perception of you based on your ability to consistently "act" in ways that validate your newly designed brand.

1. What actions and behaviors do you need to engage in to "validate" your leadership brand to important others?

When selecting your behaviors, be practical, tactical, and specific. Being practical means selecting a behavior that you know you can keep up with on a consistent basis. If you want to be known as "creating and maintaining a communication network," you may not want to commit to meeting with every member of your team on a weekly basis. That may be something that you can't keep up with. Being tactical is all about thinking strategically about each behavior that you select. Rather than being literal, think outside of the box and find ways to leverage your behaviors for maximum impact. Finally, be specific. If one of your leadership traits is most relevant to a specific employee or department, say that. You don't need to be everything to everyone. Think carefully about how each person you engage with needs to perceive you in order for you to earn the most respect and have the greatest impact.

Leadership Traits Aligned Actions

_____

_____

_____

_____

_____

_____

_____

_____

_____

_____

_____

_____

_____

_____

_____

_____

_____

_____

Anticipated Challenges

At least two of the traits related to your newly designed leadership brand should be "new" or a bit of a *stretch* for you. Maybe you've always had that leadership capability inside of you, but because of your new or aspiring role, you will show more of what you have to offer to your colleagues and peers.

In the space below, identify any and all anticipated challenges that may sabotage your ability to commit fully to your new leadership identity. Think about people who may be expecting another version of you to "show up." Think about organizational systems and structures that may undermine your efforts. Think about your own inner voice and how it may cripple your efforts to portray a new better version of your professional self.

List of Anticipated Challenges

_____

_____

_____

_____

_____

_____

_____

_____

_____

_____

_____

_____

_____

_____

_____

_____

How to Overcome Anticipated Challenges

Now that you've identified challenges that you may face as you work toward developing your leadership brand, it's time to do some creative problem solving. It won't be useful to simply name each anticipated challenge. You have to take time to identify specific actions you will take when faced with each challenge. Think about tough conversations you may have to have, accountability you may need, or even strategic allies to support and mentor you during your branding transition.

Actions to Overcome Anticipated Challenges

_____

_____

_____

_____

_____

_____

_____

_____

_____

_____

_____

_____

_____

_____

_____

_____

_____

_____

_____

_____

Remember, your leadership brand won't "stick" unless you make a conscious decision to align your behaviors with each leadership trait you've selected. Then and only then will your colleagues and peers begin to perceive you in ways that will benefit your professional bottom line. Over the next 90 days work hard to firmly establish your leadership brand. If you are successful, begin to expand and deepen your brand by adding additional traits and aligned behaviors to your daily and weekly activities.

References for Leadership Traits

Bennis, Warren, and Joan Goldsmith. *Learning to Lead: A Workbook on Becoming a Leader.* 3d ed. Cambridge, Mass.: Perseus Books Group, 2003.

Bennis, Warren, and Burt Nanis. *Leaders: Strategies for Taking Charge.* New York: Harper & Row Publishers, 1985.

Caroselli, Marlene. *Leadership Skills for Managers.* New York: McGraw-Hill, 2000.

Chapman, Elwood N. *Leadership: What Every Manager Needs to Know.* Chicago: SRA Pergamon, 1989.

Gardner, John W. *On Leadership.* New York: The Free Press, 1990.

Goleman, Daniel. "What Makes a Leader?" Chapter 1 in *Harvard Business Review on What Makes a Leader.* Cambridge, Mass.: Harvard Business School Press, 2001.

Murphy, Emmett C. *Leadership IQ: A Personal Development Process Based on a Scientific Study of a New Generation of Leaders.* New York: John Wiley & Sons, 1996.

Riggs, Donald E., and Gordon A. Sabine. "Leadership." Chapter 10 in *Libraries in the '90s: What the Leaders Expect.* Phoenix, Ariz.: Oryx Press, 1988.

Winston, Mark D., ed. *Leadership in the Library and Information Science Professions: Theory and Practice*. New York: Haworth Press, 2001.

Yukl, Gary. *Leadership in Organizations*. 5 [th] ed. Upper Saddle River, N.J.: Prentice Hall, 2002.

SECTION 2
IMPLEMENTATION GUIDE

EMOTIONAL COMPETENCE

Becoming emotionally competent is all about reflecting on your emotions and heightening your emotional awareness in different situations.

Emotional Triggers

Emotional triggers are responses to situations, events, or people that provoke a strong emotional reaction. Many times we're not aware of our triggers, which can lead to a recurring cycle of reacting poorly to the same situations over and over again.

In this section, I'd like you to start thinking about your own emotional triggers. These are the things that people say and do that get under your skin. These negative situations expose the not-so-great aspects of your emotional coping skills, and can provide valuable information that can help you better manage your emotions.

For each question below, think about the distinct thought patterns and behavior that you exhibit in professional settings when faced with ideas, people, or dynamics that trigger negative emotional responses.

1. What behaviors of others cause you to have a negative emotional reaction?

_____

_____

_____

_____

_____

_____

_____

_____

_____

_____

_____

_____

_____

_____

_____

2. What organizational dynamics cause you to have a negative emotional reaction?

_____

_____

_____

_____

_____

_____

_____

_____

_____

_____
_____
_____
_____
_____

3. How do you react to these situations? (i.e. what do you do? what do you say? who do you talk to? etc.)

_____
_____
_____
_____
_____
_____
_____
_____
_____
_____
_____
_____
_____

4. What emotions do you feel when you encounter the challenges mentioned above?

_____
_____
_____
_____
_____
_____

_____

_____

_____

_____

_____

_____

_____

_____

5. How do others react to you when you display the emotions identified above?

_____

_____

_____

_____

_____

_____

_____

_____

_____

_____

_____

_____

_____

6. In what new ways can you respond to these emotional triggers?

_____

_____

_____

_____

_____

_____

_____

_____

_____

_____

_____

_____

_____

_____

_____

_____

7. How will responding in these new ways help you gain respect, increase your influence with others, and get more results?

_____

_____

_____

_____

_____

_____

_____

_____

_____

_____

_____

_____

_____

_____

If you have difficulty identifying and naming your emotional triggers, ask a close member of your network to help you by offering their perception of how you act and react in challenging situations. This information will be a helpful part of your reflective process.

SECTION 3
IMPLEMENTATION GUIDE

CONFLICT COMPETENCE

As previously recommended, go online and take the Thomas-Kilmann Conflict Styles Inventory to identify each of your primary conflict styles. Increasing your conflict competence is all about knowing when to use each conflict style.

After you've identified your primary conflict style, take some time to reflect on the questions below.

My Conflict Style in Action

1. What types of "conflicts" are common within your organization? Think of the various stakeholders in your organization and each of their wants, needs, and obligations.

_____
_____
_____
_____
_____
_____

_____

_____

_____

_____

_____

_____

_____

_____

_____

2. What types of conflicts have you encountered in your current role? How have you managed them? (i.e. Identify people, their perspective, your perspective, and outcomes)

_____

_____

_____

_____

_____

_____

_____

_____

_____

_____

_____

_____

_____

_____

3. How can you improve the way that you handle conflict in your current role?

_____

_____

_____

_____
_____
_____
_____
_____
_____
_____
_____
_____
_____
_____

Strengthening your conflict competence will take time and lots of practice. If you're a textbook avoider, you're going to have to be proactive in addressing conflict when they arise. If you tend to collaborate with others, you may try honing your competitive side when it matters most.

Learning how to adjust your conflict style to meet the needs of the situation is a difficult task. With consistent practice and bold accountability, you can significantly upgrade your conflict competence in a matter of a few months.

SECTION 4
IMPLEMENTATION GUIDE

COMMUNICATION SKILLS

Your communication skills are critical to how you are perceived by your colleagues and peers. As with conflict competence, communication is all about assessing the situation and making a purposeful decision on how to respond.

In this section, I want you to reflect upon your personal communication goals and specific actions you can take to build upon your current communication skills.

COMMUNICATION GOALS

1. What communication fears do you currently have?

_____

_____

_____

_____

_____

_____

_____

_____

_____

_____

_____

_____

_____

_____

_____

_____

2. Where do these perceived fears stem from? (i.e. cultural rules, personal expectations, dysfunctional mindsets, etc.)

_____

_____

_____

_____

_____

_____

_____

_____

_____

_____

_____

_____

_____

_____

3. What communication goals do you have?

_____

_____

_____

_____

_____

_____

_____

_____

_____

_____

_____

_____

_____

_____

_____

4. How will these changes in your communication behavior aid in gaining respect, influencing others, and getting results in your current role?

_____

_____

_____

_____

_____

_____

_____

_____

_____

_____

_____

_____

_____

Accountability is important when it comes to making major adjustments to your communication style. Enlist a colleague or peer who you can trust to provide you with purposeful feedback as they observe your communication changes. Their role is to be a mirror for you to get a sense for how your new communication skills are being perceived by the outside world.

SECTION 5
IMPLEMENTATION GUIDE

OVERCOMING POLITICS

In this section, I want you to reflect on your current workplace to get a better sense of the important dynamics that may undermine or sabotage your efforts to have an impact as a new leader.

WHO HAS THE POWER?

1. Who has the formal and informal power within your organization? Think about people with titles, but also those who have seniority, tenure, and other forms of social power.

_____
_____
_____
_____
_____
_____
_____
_____
_____

_____

_____

_____

_____

_____

_____

2. How can their formal and informal power have a negative impact on what you're trying to accomplish as a leader?

_____

_____

_____

_____

_____

_____

_____

_____

_____

_____

_____

_____

3. Who do you need to align yourself with?

_____

_____

_____

_____

_____

_____

_____

_____

_____

_____

_____

_____

_____

_____

4. How will aligning yourself with these important others help you gain respect, influence others, and get results?

_____

_____

_____

_____

_____

_____

_____

_____

_____

_____

_____

_____

_____

_____

5. What dysfunctional organizational norms could have a negative impact on what you're trying to accomplish as a leader?

_____

_____

_____

_____

_____

_____

_____

_____

_____

_____

_____

_____

_____

_____

_____

_____

6. What can you do to mitigate any planned or unplanned efforts to sabotage your leadership plans?

_____

_____

_____

_____

_____

_____

_____

_____

_____

_____

_____

_____

_____

_____

Politics are a part of the DNA or any organization. One person… even a few people cannot significantly change the dysfunctions of an organization. Your role is to become aware of power dynamics, potential threats, and important others who may derail your leadership efforts. Your focus needs to be on navigating any organizational dysfunctions with agility and poise. Don't get discouraged, rather see this as an opportunity for you to strengthen and refine your skills as a leader.

SECTION 6
IMPLEMENTATION GUIDE

HOW TO "PUT IN WORK"

After identifying your weaknesses, setting goals, and making a plan, you have *almost* everything you need to be successful as a new leader. The last thing that separates average leaders from phenomenal leaders is the amount of consistent effort that is put in over time to refine and develop their skills.

Putting in work is less about quantity and more about quality. Many leaders are so overwhelmed working in their organizations that they neglect to work on themselves. Create a consistent habit to evaluate your leadership skills on a monthly basis. Get feedback, change your behavior, assess your results, and do it all over again.

In this section, I want you to reflect on how you can create purposeful habits to hold yourself accountable along your journey as a leader.

My Put in Work Plan

1. What current habits must I remove from my daily routine to become more effective as a leader?

_____

_____

_____

_____

_____

_____

_____

_____

_____

_____

_____

_____

_____

_____

2. What new habits do I need to add to my daily routine to become more effective as a leader?

_____

_____

_____

_____

_____

_____

_____

_____

_____

_____
_____
_____
_____
_____

3. What negative mindsets do I need to release to become more effective as a leader?

_____
_____
_____
_____
_____
_____
_____
_____
_____
_____
_____
_____

4. What new mindsets do I need to establish to become more effective as a leader?

_____
_____
_____
_____
_____
_____
_____
_____

_____

_____

_____

_____

_____

_____

Remember, the practice of reestablishing goals and habits is an ongoing process that should happen once or twice a year. What you identify here should be put into practice immediately and within several months you should be ready to move to the next level of reflection.

IMPLEMENTATION GUIDE BONUS

NETWORKING

Networking outside of your organization is important, but as a new leader, networking from within your organization needs to be your top priority.

In this section, take some time to reflect on key stakeholders within your organization and how they can help you gain respect, influence others, and get results.

Identify Your Internal Network

1. Who are potential mentors within your current organization? How could they facilitate your leadership agenda?

_____

_____

_____

_____

_____

_____

_____

_____

_____

_____

_____

_____

_____

_____

_____

2. Who has formal or informal influence within your organization? How can you leverage their social status to facilitate your leadership agenda?

_____

_____

_____

_____

_____

_____

_____

_____

_____

_____

_____

_____

_____

_____

_____

_____

3. What events or meetings could you attend to build strategic relationships within your organization and industry?

_____

_____

_____

_____

_____

_____

_____

_____

_____

_____

_____

_____

_____

_____

4. What can you do to build social capital and become a resource to others in your organization?

_____

_____

_____

_____

_____

_____

_____

_____

_____

_____

_____

_____

_____

_____

_____

_____

Networking is something that should be purposeful and strategic. Remember not to focus on how many people you know, but the quality of the relationships you build. The easiest way to build professional relationships is to position yourself as a resource. Take some time each month to figure out how you can be a resource to the most influential people in your network.